Habits *of the* Disciplined

Bestselling author **Steven Schuster** has always been captivated by the intricacies of the human mind. From the echoing hallways of libraries to the serene landscapes of the Rocky Mountains, Steven has ventured far and wide in his relentless quest for knowledge and first-hand experience. Blending profound psychological insights with captivating storytelling, he has reached readers across the globe, igniting their passion for self-discovery.

A self-proclaimed 'eternal student', Steven spends his days immersed in a medley of fictional prose and cutting-edge research, distilling wisdom that spans different fields of study.

When he's not penning transformative books, you'll find Steven exploring a hidden forest trail, indulging in his love for vintage jazz, or lost in deep conversation with fellow thinkers at quaint cafés from Paris to Kuala Lumpur.

Join Steven on a journey into the depths of consciousness, and emerge with knowledge that help you live your best life.

Other Books by the Author

Discipline Your Thoughts

Rewire Your Mind

The Critical Thinker

Mindset Makeover

The Perfection Trap

Habits *of the* Disciplined
Positive Changes for Your Mind and Soul

STEVEN SCHUSTER

Published by
Rupa Publications India Pvt. Ltd 2025
7/16, Ansari Road, Daryaganj
New Delhi 110002

Sales centres:
Bengaluru Chennai
Hyderabad Jaipur Kathmandu
Kolkata Mumbai Prayagraj

Copyright © Steven Schuster 2025
Published under arrangement with Steven Schuster
through TLL Literary Agency

The views and opinions expressed in this book are the author's own and the facts are as reported by him which have been verified to the extent possible, and the publishers are not in any way liable for the same.

All rights reserved.
No part of this publication may be reproduced, transmitted, or stored in a retrieval system, in any form or by any means, electronic, mechanical, photocopying, recording or otherwise, without the prior permission of the publisher.

P-ISBN: 978-93-5702-669-7
E-ISBN: 978-93-5702-726-7

First impression 2025

10 9 8 7 6 5 4 3 2 1

The moral right of the author has been asserted.

Printed in India

This book is sold subject to the condition that it shall not, by way of trade or otherwise, be lent, resold, hired out, or otherwise circulated, without the publisher's prior consent, in any form of binding or cover other than that in which it is published.

Contents

1. How Are Habits Created? — 1
2. Why Habits? — 10
3. Jump off the Expectation Train — 17
4. Self-Discipline — 22
5. Procrastination — 26
6. Productivity Booster Habits — 34
7. Practice Moderation — 41
8. Forget Multi-Tasking — 49
9. Happiness Boosters — 55
10. Success Habits — 63
11. Habits of a Good Life — 75
12. The Stoic Way to a Good Life — 82

Final Words — 89
Reference — 90
Endnotes — 94

1
How Are Habits Created?

Habits are front and center in the self-development industry now. We all want to learn how to master good habits and shed the bad ones. However, many people have only a vague idea about which habits are truly helpful and needed the most. They often divide their focus and devote their energy to many small habits with low leverage instead of focusing on a few crucial, 'keystone' habits that jumpstart positive, high-leverage life changes. This book will help you discover these meaningful and powerful habits that can help you make the changes you're looking for in your life.

First we need to understand what a habit is. We create a habit when we repeatedly behave the same way as a response to a stimulus or cue in our environment. Our responses become automatic over time. Why? Because when we automatically respond to familiar cues we can expend a lot less mental energy, allowing our mind to focus on other things. The brain is a busy organ and by nature looks for shortcuts to ease its workload; it loves being in a power-saving mode.

"The average adult human brain weighs only 2 percent of a person's total body weight. However, it demands roughly 20 percent of our resting metabolic rate (RMR)—the total amount of energy our bodies expend in one very lazy day of no activity. RMR varies from person to person depending on age, gender, size, and health. A typical adult human brain runs on around 12 watts—a fifth of the power required by a standard 60 watt lightbulb, if you convert from calories appropriately."[1]

If we take the standard RMR, we need to consume 2,000 calories to function well. The brain eats up 20% of that total, which is 400 calories. That is about 16.66 calories per hour or 0.26 calories per minute. This number covers all functions of the brain, not just its thinking process.

The brain does everything in its power to turn every repeating pattern in our life into a habit. If we are not vigilant and mindful about this tendency of our brain, it will be successful. In most cases, this process is indeed a success—by turning processes into automatic habits, our brain is released to think constantly of basic behaviors like talking, choosing what clothing items we need to wear every day, and so on.

Charles Duhigg, the author of the book *The Power of Habit*, writes about numerous research studies on how habits are formed, maintained, and how they can be broken. His research shows that habits are made up of three parts: a cue in the environment, a behavioral response or action, and a reward (this may also be the removal of something unpleasant).[2]

The habit loop:

Cue ⟶ Behavior ⟶ Reward

Duhigg's habit loop can be understood by even the youngest humans. In our house, from the time my children were toddlers, they knew that as soon as they put their pajamas on (cue), they needed to brush their teeth (behavior) in order to have story time before bed (reward). This became their nightly habit, or routine, and we held fast to it. There were no more battles about brushing teeth in our house because the habit became ingrained in them as the cue was consistent every night and it always resulted in something they loved—reading books together.

The habits we'd like to break follow the same pattern of cue, behavior, and reward. For example, if you are prone to overindulging on food, your desire to eat may not come from feelings of hunger, but rather may be triggered by the aroma of your favorite foods baking in the oven, watching others eat dessert, or a feeling of boredom as you watch

TV. The brain starts craving the food, remembers how tasty that baked good is. The cue then triggers your behavior of eating even when you aren't necessarily hungry. Once you eat your baked good, a rush of pleasure runs through your system; your brain rewards you by improving your mood, lessening your boredom, or creating a sense of comfort as you associate the baked good with positive memories, not to mention satisfying your taste buds. This is how habits work.

Habit researchers have found that if we hope to create new habits, or break old ones, our focus should be on the cue more than the behavior. We tend to put all of our time and energy into creating a new behavior or eliminating a troubling one. We miss the opportunity to put our willpower to work more effectively by better understanding our cues which will increase the likelihood of reacting differently, forming helpful habits or altering our existing environmental cues so that we can eliminate our negative and unhealthy habits.

Creating new environmental cues can greatly improve our chances of forming permanent positive habits. For example, perhaps you want to improve your chaotic morning routine where everyone feels rushed and you end up running late or leaving home without something important. Instead of focusing on a behavior in the morning, you could decide to put your energy into developing a new cue that will ultimately lead to a positive and more efficient habit and routine. It may not seem like a big deal, but this little change in mindset and focus can make a world of difference. A classic example of a morning habit cue change is putting your running pants and shoes on right after you brush your teeth. This way, doing that 15-minute morning run will be easier. Frankly, you already invested energy in the process of putting on your equipment, you can't let that effort go to waste.

One of the easiest ways to create a new habit is to work with a cue that already exists in your everyday life. In our house, it was family dinner. We always talked about our day at the dinner table, so we built upon that. At the end of dinner, we went around the table and we each shared one thing from our day we were thankful for. Then we shared what the next day had in store for us in terms of activities we had planned. That got everything fresh in all of our minds so that once everyone finished sharing, we immediately got up from the table and laid out our clothes for the next day, along with anything else we might need for work, school, or extracurricular activities. Once we had everything organized and accessible for the morning, we returned to the table to clean up our dishes.

It wasn't long before our table talks automatically triggered our preparations for the next day. It became second nature. It was our family's habit. It took very little time and effort, and we began to feel that when circumstances came up that caused us to miss this routine, something was off and we actually missed doing it.

The only thing missing from our example is the reward component. While a less rushed and stressful morning routine was enough of a reward on its own for my wife and me, it took a little extra for our kids. We decided to set a timer each morning and record the amount of time that we saved every day with our new routine. On Saturday, we would add all of the time together and spend that amount of time doing a fun activity as a family.

Sometimes we even turned it into a little challenge, and if we saved more time than the week before, we would double the amount of time we spent playing on the weekend. This reward further cemented our children's dedication to our new family habit, and we have never looked back.

Identifying cues however is not always easy. One can't change something one doesn't know, right? Duhigg explains that if you want to identify the cue of your bad habit you should start to think about the five Ws:

- When the habit will occur;
- Where you will be;
- Who else will be around;
- What you are doing; and
- What your mental state is

For example, I used to have the bad habit of binge eating. According to the bullet points above, I started paying attention to myself. After a few days of observing my actions, I realized that my cravings usually kicked in around 8 to 9 pm. I usually have early dinner around 6 pm and after that I prefer not to eat anything substantial. Around 8 pm is when I sit down to either read or watch TV in my study. In my case there is no one around. And my mental state could be defined as idle to slightly bored. After profound observation and analysis I realized that my main reward I'm seeking with binge eating is in fact socializing with my family. When I understood that my craving was more about company than food it was easier to change my behavior. Instead of going to the fridge, I stopped in the living room and started chatting with my wife or kids. Sometimes I called them to join me in my study to watch TV. Before I knew it, I didn't feel the craving for food anymore.

When your goal is to change a habit, think of yourself as a detective trying to find clues about why you are repeating the unhealthy habit and how badly it affects your life. It is when you solve this mystery that you will be able to change your actions to more positive ones. Focusing on the cue by reflecting on the five Ws we discussed will find the cues that are consistently triggering your behavior.

Our habits, good and bad, become a comfort to us because we can rely on them. The important thing is to remember that habits are created, not born. They all start with a craving that sends signals to our brain through a cue; it is time to begin the habit. The process concludes with a reward—something that is pleasant to our brain therefore it signals we should repeat the habit in the future.

The European Journal of Social Psychology published a study which followed 96 people over 12 weeks to find out how long it can take to go from starting a new habit to the point where it feels automatic and lasting. The results showed that the average time it took the participants was 66 days. This should give us all hope that if we are willing to put in the work and commit ourselves, we too can change our habits—it will just be a matter of time.[3]

Contemplate about the following two practices. Use them as guidance to solidify the keystone habits you would like to change or adopt for yourself.

(a) There are certain things we can do which will increase our odds of adopting lasting habits in our lives. First, we can share our habit goal out loud with those around us and ask them for their help in keeping us on track. Asking them to point it out to us if we revert to our old habit will increase our awareness and make us more accountable. No one likes to disappoint people they care about, and we will be more likely to stick with our plan.

(b) We need to reflect on the deep, and sometimes unconscious reasons we want to change our habits and how we expect this change to impact our life; we should remind ourselves about our expected rewards. This will become our source of persistence when things get difficult. Have a powerful vision about what kind of person you want to be; what kind of activities you want in your life; and what kind of relationship you want.

Key Habit Takeaway of This Chapter:

Focus on the cue that triggers your habit rather than the behavior itself. Have a vision of who you want to be and where you want your habit change to take you.

2

Why Habits?

You bought this book with the specific intent to change your life. This change may be a clear goal in your mind like starting a new career, finding a new partner, or improving the work or relationship you already have. You may think that the key to all this is adopting some better habits.

Good habits smooth the road of life, that's true. But focusing purely on achieving external things by changing a habit won't bring lasting fulfillment unless we start with changing the way we think about ourselves. Pin it as habit nr. 1. Change your self-perception. It doesn't matter how productive you become; if your inner monologue consists only of berating and self-loathing, becoming more productive won't take you to a better place. You won't feel happier or more fulfilled in life.

Similarly, adopting only the habit of having a general

positive self-perception won't take you to a better place. You might be more positive about life, which is a good thing, but you won't live up to your full potential and won't put more food on the table.

Habits targeting your external and internal circumstances should be adopted and evolved in balance.

People often get stuck when they decide to change their lives. It is difficult to figure out what area of life needs to change the most, as well as where to start or what to do.

Do what you can now, based on where you are now, with what you have now. Do something. Do anything. Don't stay stuck at the same place. There is no "right time", "enough knowledge", or "sufficient motivation" to start working on a new habit.

I may risk saying that the first good habit, the one all other habits mount on, is the habit of doing.

The life changes you're hoping for won't come from some deep, highly motivated place from within. Motivation burns out much quicker than any habit that's taken a strong root. Don't rely and depend on motivation.

Your actions will create the change.

Your ability to sit down (or stand up) and take consistent action towards your habit change will make or break its realization. You need to take action in the sunshine, in the rain, in health, in sickness, in a foul mood, when you are over the moon, when your mom comes to visit, when you cut your finger during cooking… only then will your new habits take root and your life will take the turn you want.

People usually look at taking action as the consequence of motivation, not vice versa. But they feel motivated only in certain, emotionally charged moments. This is why most people don't accomplish what they want.

How many times did you start learning a craft, let's say, because you were inspired by someone? Or because you were afraid of the negative consequences? For example, I started learning the piano because I felt inspired by one of my coworkers who played it flawlessly and could entertain his students with it. Every time I heard him play, I was fired up for a few days to practice my piano skills and then I started slacking off. When I didn't hear my coworker play for a long time, I lost motivation. When the object of my inspiration was not present and I also didn't harness quite the reward I was expecting (my piano skills were less advanced than my coworker's, thus the cheers I got for my efforts were proportionately less as well) I lost interest in practicing playing the piano.

If I wanted to illustrate this process on a cause-effect graph, it would look like this:

Inspiration ⟶ Motivation ⟶ Action

As you can see in my example, this approach is not the best way to master a new skill or adopt a new habit. The first mistake I made was that the internal and external rewards of adopting this habit were not in balance; I wanted to learn the piano for purely external reasons. I didn't care about how much this would give me personally, all I was focusing on was the success I might harness from other people's feedback. I didn't get the feedback I expected so what happened? I quit. I lost motivation and I had no further reason to continue my practice. I didn't have a *why* for myself. Keep this in mind, we'll talk about the importance of *why* later.

The other problem was that my want to learn the piano was inspired by a negative emotion: I was envious of my coworker for stealing all the attention just by sitting down playing an instrument. I wanted that attention for myself.

Negative emotions often fuel us more to change than positive ones. For example, we want to become more patient because we want to escape the negative consequences of our impatience. We are not motivated to become more patient to make others feel safer. We want to communicate better because we hate enduring the devastating impact of a verbal misunderstanding.

When a negative event happens, we pledge to change. But at the same time, we are sabotaged by other negative emotions that are the byproduct of the situation we wish to fix. Impatience attracts resentment and irritation that we attribute to the other person so we might think, *Why should I be more patient with him? He pissed me off.*

Miscommunication attracts defensiveness, a feeling of inadequacy, anger, or shame that may keep us away from trying to improve.

When you think of adopting a good habit, first make sure that:

- You want to change for internal and external reasons equally; and
- You are focusing on the positive outcome of the habit change (on what you are getting instead of what you want to avoid)

When you are sure that your habit goals are clear and unaffected by any negative force, change the order of the graph elements like this:

Action ⟶ Inspiration ⟶ Motivation

Take action first. Do something for yourself, to achieve your goal.

Just by sitting down for ten minutes, doing what you need to do you may get inspired. Want to write a book? Great. You don't feel inspired? No problem. Sit down and start typing ideas for your book in the next ten minutes. Maybe one of these ideas will trigger a spark of inspiration in you. The inspiration gained through taking action will give you enough motivation to finish what you need to do for the day.

Why Habits?

The "do something" habit is as simple and as hard as this.

For example, now—right now—when I started writing this chapter I was utterly unmotivated. It is a bright, beautiful afternoon, my kids are playing outside, my wife is firing up the barbecue... and here I am, in my study, hunching over the computer trying to write this book. I sat down to do it for no other reason than I know for a fact, and out of many years of practice, that I will get in the zone after about ten minutes of work. And so I did. By the time you read these lines I was typing like a robot, my brain was invaded with more ideas than the speed of my fingers could capture. I will go on now with the habit of doing.

When you commit to adopt a new habit, know this: the road won't be easy. In order to get motivated, you need to get inspired. To get inspired, you need to take action. Do something.

Take action, get inspired, get fired up, work, repeat. Take action, get inspired, get fired up, work, repeat. You get it.

The more often you practice the "do something" habit, the more you'll believe that you are actually able to do whatever you need to do. You will see clearly that whenever you say you're not quite in the zone now that it's rather an excuse instead of an actual obstacle.

You want to do something but you don't quite know what? Is the goal too big to just randomly do something?

No problem. Do this, then: break the goal down into smaller and smaller steps. A monthly goal to a weekly, a weekly goal to a daily, a daily goal to an hourly. Do you know what you need to do in the next hour? Then do something about it now.

My mother used to say that if you don't know how to solve a problem, write down alternative solutions; the more you think about it the more and better answers you'll get. I don't know what goal, habit change, you have in your mind but I know this. By simply sitting down, brainstorming possible first steps is already a "doing" habit. Instead of looking up at the sky, hoping for help, you'll actually get closer to what you need to do. The action of thinking about first steps will inspire you with new ideas and insights.

Change is less dependent on knowledge and motivation than it is on taking action based on the knowledge you have.

Key Habit Takeaway of This Chapter:

Do something. Do anything. Take action and get inspired.

3

Jump off the Expectation Train

Do you ever find yourself wishing you could return to the simpler time of your childhood? It's ironic that when we were children we couldn't wait to grow up, but once we became adults we found that it isn't quite all that easy and cool as we thought, and then we get nostalgic for the less complicated moments of our youth.

Why is this? It turns out that there is a simple reason behind it.

Perhaps our lives were so much simpler as children because the expectations for us were clear. If we listened to our parents and teachers and did what they expected of us, we knew we would be rewarded in a certain way.

Author Mark Manson refers to this as the "Algorithmic Life." He says if you do X, you are rewarded with Y. The X is the expectation, and it was given clearly to you as a child. The Y is the reward or result, and it was something you could count on and expect because it was dependable. During this time, life was predictable. There are of course exceptions to this statement, for some children—especially those whose parents had substance abuse problems—life was not so consistent. For argument's sake, let's look at the average family habits where the Algorithmic Life structure applies.[1]

The Algorithmic Life is fine as long as it works, but as we get older, we find that it doesn't always hold true. Life isn't always predictable or fair, and some of the things we were taught don't always turn out to be accurate. For example, we are often taught that going to a good college is vital to our career success, when many people find successful employment in businesses that are less concerned with diplomas than we would think.

When the Algorithmic Life falls apart, there may be additional unanticipated problems that manifest as well. People who have spent their lives only trying to meet others' expectations may find that they do not feel they have an identity of their own. They may have relied on others to tell them what they should work toward and care about for so long that they aren't sure what they are passionate about pursuing in their life now. They may enter into relationships with certain expectations and think in terms of what they will get from the relationship instead of having healthy relationships. They can easily become disenchanted and miserable when the expectations they hold aren't met.

Some people go on to be so discouraged when the Algorithmic Life falls apart that they think they shouldn't make the mistake of having any positive expectations in life because they only lead to disappointment. They adopt a negative outlook on the world so that they may try to protect themselves from experiencing those feelings again. Having unreasonably low expectations of life is just as harmful and unhealthy as having unreasonably high ones.

The Algorithmic Life may be a helpful method of teaching children, but since life doesn't really work that way in reality, adults should leave the expectations set by the Algorithmic Life behind them. Manson says that "possibly the most important skill one can develop in one's own life is how to act without expectation." He points out that it can create a sense of freedom that allows you to follow your passions without relying on merely extrinsic rewards. You can enter into relationships and unconditionally love others. You aren't held back by a fear of failure and can be more creative.

The second keystone habit I'd like to introduce you to is living and acting with reasonable expectations.

Without unreasonable expectations constraining you, you are better equipped to deal with disappointment in life, and you can be more open-minded about changing your beliefs as you learn new things. It will take time and practice, but you will gain confidence in your ability to handle whatever life throws at you. Letting go of the Algorithmic Life and the unreasonable expectations that go along with it will set you free, allowing you to live a more productive and fulfilling life.

There is scientific proof to back up the connection between lowering your expectations and being happy. The University College of London recently completed a study of MRIs showing a link between happiness and lower but reasonable expectations. The study's author and neuroscientist Dr. Robb Rutledge stated, "Happiness depends not on how well things are going, but whether things are going better or worse than expected." He added, "It is often said that you will be happier if your expectations are lower. We find that there is some truth to this: Lower expectations make it more likely that an outcome will exceed those expectations and have a positive impact on happiness."[2]

There is another school of thought which suggests that it is possible to set your expectations too low, demonstrating that you don't value yourself enough. It is important to distinguish between different types of low expectations.

One type of low expectations is rooted in low self-esteem and a poor sense of self-worth. If low expectations are set because you feel unworthy or undeserving, then those low expectations are certainly a bad habit and should not be subscribed to as they can be detrimental.

The other type of low expectations, the one which includes reality checking and setting reasonable expectations, can be a good habit to form. These low expectations involve having a realistic view of life and not allowing our mood to suffer when expectations aren't met. This line of thinking promotes the idea that we should hope for the best, but prepare for the worst.

Having lower but reasonable expectations, we don't have to struggle so much to try to make ourselves happy. We will be able to be pleasantly surprised by the little things and find that happiness is all around us.

This is not to say that we should never aim high. Being realistic and having a desire to improve your life does not need to be mutually exclusive. It is possible for both thoughts to peacefully coexist in our lives.

Key Habit Takeaway of This Chapter:

Have healthy and realistic expectations. "Happiness depends not on how well things are going, but whether things are going better or worse than expected."

4
Self-Discipline

Discipline Is Inherently Hard

Oddly enough, we often see our future self as another person, which can contribute to our difficulty in being disciplined as we try to achieve our goals in the present. Science backs this up. In one study, researchers asked the participants to think about their current self, to think about a celebrity like Natalie Portman or Matt Damon, and to think about themselves in ten years. They scanned the participants' brains as they did their thinking and found that the scans were almost exactly the same when they thought about their future selves as when they thought about the celebrity (a stranger).

Jason Mitchell from Harvard University also found that when people imagine themselves experiencing something enjoyable a year from now, many people use the same brain areas that they do when they think of a stranger.[1]

This may help us to understand why people may be willing to behave in self-destructive ways in the present while giving little thought to the consequences those actions may have for their lives in the future. This brings to mind all of the warnings we try to give to young adults that their social media posts and online interactions now can have a big impact on their lives later on when their future employers look at their behavior. All too often, they experience a disconnect between their present and future selves and lack self-discipline. Our warnings go unheeded, leading to difficult consequences.

Scientific Methods to Increase Discipline

A joint study was conducted at the Hong Kong University of Science and the University of Chicago which found that if students were asked to remember a time when they resisted temptation, 70 percent of them indulged in temptation at their next opportunity. But if the question was changed to ask them to remember *why* they resisted temptation, 69 percent of the students resisted the temptation. This seems to suggest that one way to improve your self-discipline is to remind yourself of the reason that you want to resist giving in.[2]

Another study gave some hope to many who struggle to find the self-discipline needed to resist the temptation to use drugs. It found that adults who were recovering from drug abuse had reduced cravings and depression after they participated in deliberate, slow breathing for twenty minutes. We can certainly apply this technique to give our self-discipline a boost in many other areas of our lives as well.

Northwestern University conducted a study of forty adults in romantic relationships by separating them into three groups. The first group was encouraged to use their non-dominant hand when they brushed their teeth. The second group was encouraged to start saying "yes" instead of "yeah." The third group acted as the control group and wasn't given any instruction at all.

After two weeks of participation, the first two groups displayed fewer tendencies to get angry or violent with their romantic partners while the third group exhibited no change in this behavior. While there doesn't seem to be a natural connection between what they were asked to do and the ultimate results, by simply being more conscious in even one area of their lives, there was an impact in other areas as well. It may seem like a small thing, but being mindful forced their brains to pause and make a choice to do the harder thing instead of the easier one. In this case, their brains paused and decided to stay calm (harder) rather than reacting with anger to something that upset them (easier).

When we choose to be mindful, we are making the conscious choice to be aware and present in the moment. We are choosing to be focused. Being mindful is a way of life. It helps us to reach our goals and dreams by increasing our self-discipline. Without self-discipline, our habits and dreams are little more than wishful thinking, and we are no closer to achieving them. We are the only ones we can rely upon to create the lives we want for ourselves, not some external source of inspiration and motivation.

Key Habit Takeaway of This Chapter:

Practice improving your self-discipline muscle.

5

Procrastination

What is it about our minds that allows, if not encourages, us to put off things that actually matter to us? Psychologists would classify procrastination as a lapse in self-control which leads one to choose behaviors that allow them to avoid a stressful or boring task in the short term.

Researchers have identified different types of procrastinators and also the reasons why and how these types of people procrastinate.

Arousal Procrastinators

Arousal procrastinators get a rush of adrenaline from waiting until the last minute to complete a task. They are the people who brag that they do their best work while under pressure to meet a deadline. These procrastinators are almost addicted to the feeling they get from the adrenaline rush, and their motivation to complete a task is panic.[1]

An example of an arousal procrastinator is someone who knows they have guests coming to visit for weeks, but avoids cleaning the house until just a few hours before the guests are due to arrive.

Arousal procrastinators may want to try to finish a task early and see if they feel just as good if they are able to give themselves a few hours off to just relax as they do when they rely on the rush of adrenaline.

Avoidant Procrastinators

A second type of procrastinator is the avoidant procrastinator. This person doesn't want to face an unpleasant task and will attempt to avoid it at all costs. These procrastinators may fear the task in front of them, so they put it off.

An example of an avoidant procrastinator is someone who may delay having a conversation with their boss asking for a raise or some vacation time because they dread the thought of an uncomfortable experience.

Avoidant procrastinators may want to keep in mind that they think they are postponing a task in order to calm themselves, to give themselves space to build up the courage to face it—but in reality, the task is still very much on their mind, perhaps even on an unconscious level. They may be better served to think of facing the task as being like ripping off a Band-Aid. It may hurt for a bit, but it will be better off in the long run to get it over with quickly.

Indecisive Procrastinators

Indecisive procrastinators are people who feel overwhelmed by a task to the point that they may be frozen and thus not even know where to begin. They may be perfectionists who are worried about making the wrong choice or giving up on a better option, so they are somewhat paralyzed and decide that putting off making a choice for as long as possible is the best way to go.

An example of an indecisive procrastinator may be a person who is planning a party, but they have so many items on their to-do list that they don't know what to do first. When it comes time to make final decisions about the cake, decorations, presents, etc., it is like they are stuck in quicksand and unable to move.

Indecisive procrastinators may do well to remember that just because they make a decision about a task, it doesn't mean it has to be set in stone. It is possible to go back and change their mind at a later time and make adjustments to their plans.

Most of us are not just one type of procrastinator, but

rather a combination of all three.

There is a battle going on in our brain every day. In one corner is the limbic system, the unconscious zone of our brain which includes the pleasure center, while in the other corner is the prefrontal cortex, home to our internal planning center. When the limbic system is victorious, which is quite a regular occurrence, we find ourselves procrastinating and putting tasks off. Our brain is wired to seek pleasure and avoid uncomfortable situations, and it all happens in our subconscious mind.[2]

Before you are tempted to say that procrastinating is something that is out of your control, it's time to reclaim your power once again. Making decisions is a voluntary process, which means we can control it. What you do depends on what identity you choose for yourself to follow. If your identity is something like, *I can't finish stuff on time because I'm a procrastinator*, or a cricket, guess what? Your brain will make sure it proves you right. Stop telling yourself that you are something you don't want to be. Rewrite your brain's programming, raise the standards you have for yourself. The brain, as lazy as it is, just wants to stay consistent with your thoughts. Remember, staying consistent is your brain's main aim: to avoid cognitive dissonance. So when you say you're a procrastinator, your brain will go along with this thought. If you tell yourself, "I finish all my tasks on time and I do a high-quality job,"

Habits of the Disciplined

your brain will aid you to do just that. It's as simple and as hard as this.[3]

Besides understanding the work of our brain on the level of our thoughts, we also need to understand how the brain functions on a biological level.

We need to back up the standards we set for ourselves with activities that make that standard happen. When we get distracted from what our standard is and we aren't present in the moment and focused on the task in front of us, our limbic system will take the opportunity to seize control. Then the chance that we will give in to what feels good increases.

A dose of dopamine goes hand-in-hand with procrastination, and it makes us feel better. This part of our brain can quickly send out an emotional reaction in just a small fraction of a second, while the more practical prefrontal cortex takes three full seconds to activate. This would mean that the logical part of our brain usually wouldn't stand a chance in overcoming the pleasure center, but knowledge is power. Understanding how this process works allows us to exert our own control over it rather than being helpless.

The limbic system is a dominant part of our brain that is always at work and is completely developed from the time we are born. It controls our basic emotions as well as our moods and instincts. The limbic system encourages us to avoid unpleasant situations. Sometimes that can be helpful, like telling us to pull our hand away from a hot stove, but other times it may hinder our progress, like in the instance of enabling us to procrastinate.

The prefrontal cortex is not a dominant part of our brain. It is where we put information together and make decisions. This is the part of the brain that will ultimately be the driving force for us to get stuff done. The prefrontal cortex doesn't work automatically—it requires effort on our part to help this section of our brain to do its job.

The amygdala is the part of the brain that is involved in procrastination. We seem to procrastinate largely because we want to protect ourselves from negative feelings and failure. The amygdala helps to regulate our feelings, decision-making capabilities, memory, and fears. It also influences our "fight-or-flight" response. We typically think of this as being used when we sense that we are in some type of physical danger, but it can happen within our minds too. If we start to feel stressed out and overwhelmed by a task, the amygdala releases the fight-or-flight response in an attempt to protect us from panic and stress. This part of the brain is also responsible for releasing adrenaline, which can slow down the calculating and practical prefrontal cortex and make way for the impulsive pleasure center of the limbic system to take over, making you think procrastinating is a good idea in the moment.

Dopamine is produced by pleasant experiences. Our bodies like dopamine so much that our brains are constantly looking to repeat activities that are pleasurable and avoiding the others just so that we can experience the feeling of more dopamine. Dopamine encourages us to avoid things we perceive make us feel bad while encouraging us to do things we perceive will make us feel good.

All of this may seem insurmountable, but don't worry, there is hope for us yet. Kenneth McGraw conducted a research, which found the biggest obstacle to success is often just getting started. Further research on this topic discovered that we tend to procrastinate on large tasks because we fixate on the worst parts and then put off getting started.

One possible solution to help us overcome this obstacle is the 10-minute rule to beat procrastination. If you can commit to doing something for just 10 minutes, it will get you up and moving to get started. It's possible to do nearly anything for 10 minutes. It makes the task seem much less overwhelming and daunting. If you are tempted to stop after only 10 minutes, try to commit to continuing for at least another 10 minutes. Set the goals in manageable chunks of 10 minutes at a time just to keep your momentum going. Before you know it, you just might have finished the task you've been putting off.

It may be true that our brains are wired in a way that makes us predisposed to procrastinate, but that doesn't mean we should give in and just resign ourselves to being helpless and unable to avoid it. Now we have a greater understanding of the way our brains work, and we are equipped with tools that can help us overcome any obstacles that stand in our way.

> **Key Habit Takeaway of This Chapter:**
>
> Our brain is prone to aid us with procrastination. But we don't need to choose to procrastinate. The hard part is getting started. Commit to do what you need to do just for 10 minutes. Before you know it, you'll get in the zone.

6

Productivity Booster Habits

Would you like to be able to squeeze even more out of your days than you already do? I have yet to meet someone who thinks that 24 hours in a day is enough time to accomplish everything they would like to, while still having time to relax and enjoy being with their favorite people doing their favorite things. While there is unfortunately no way to extend the amount of time we have to work with, luckily for us, there are some things we can do to help us get more bang for our buck with the time we do have.

The first step toward achieving more productivity in our lives is to track the things we do.

Researchers have found that when they look at how effective a specific intervention is, the participants who were encouraged to track their progress were most likely to show improvement regardless of what the intervention was. For example, when people wear a pedometer, on average, they walk an extra mile or more a day and increase their activity levels by approximately 27 percent.[1]

What does this mean for you? You can channel these findings into your own life and take advantage of the situation by tracking your time. If you shine a light on exactly how it is that you spend your time each day, your increased awareness will automatically cause you to waste less time and use the time you have to focus more on the things you value most.

How does this work? You won't stop wanting to waste time. The average human prefers doing relaxing things that are not the most productive use of their time. However, much of the time waste is not made up of highly pleasurable activities, rather mind-numbing ones that don't really charge people in any way. Once we identify and track what we spend our time on and for how long, the most wasteful things will act as a deterrent for us to at least make an effort and do something valuable. Also, who wants to track wasted time? Tracking our time is already hard work so we'll be less inclined to invest this hard work in nonsensical activities. From this point to becoming actually productive is a very small step. The more productive activities you can track in your day the more proud you'll feel. This pride can easily trigger a "today's maximum is tomorrow's minimum" mindset which, if kept between healthy boundaries, can be very rewarding.

Productive people know that if something isn't worth tracking, it's simply not worth doing. Make an accountability chart to record the productive things you have completed during the day. You'll be able to actually see how much you are really accomplishing, and you'll be well on your way to a more productive you.

I'm a list person. Whether it is a grocery list, a to-do list, I'm down for them. I sometimes joke that I need a list to keep track of my lists. I rely on my lists to keep me focused, diligent, and productive. I like them because they keep me on track, but also because they are a visual record of the things I have already accomplished during my day. For a long time, I thought it was just my strange fascination with my lists guiding me, but there is actually research out there that backs me up.

It turns out that we should especially track our small victories. They may not seem like much to us, but to our brains, they are actually a very big deal. Our brains are hardwired to be more sensitive to bad news and negativity. This is so automatic that it begins as soon as our brains start to process information.

John Cacioppo, Ph.D. at the University of Chicago, conducted a study while he was at Ohio State University. He showed people pictures of things that were connected to positive feelings (like images of delicious foods or fancy cars), pictures of things that would create negative feelings (like images of an injured animal or a sad child), and pictures of things that could be expected to cause neutral feelings (like images of a lamp or a glass). He then measured the electrical activity that occurred in the participants' cerebral cortexes. He found that there is a greater surge of electrical activity and a stronger reaction in the brain when people are exposed to things they perceive as being negative. This demonstrates that bad news has a far greater impact on us than good news.[2]

Our tendency to put so much weight and emphasis on negative things came about for a good purpose in the past—trying to protect ourselves from harm. From the beginning of our history, our very survival had to be our top priority. Our brains had to develop in such a way that we had to always be on guard, aware, and ready to respond to danger.

We can use our tracking to overpower our negativity bias. It turns out that I'm not alone in enjoying crossing things off my to-do lists. We get tiny dopamine spikes when we cross things off our list whether the items are big or small. If we keep a daily list of accomplishments or even just a to-do list, we can track all of the positive things we complete in our day. The more positivity shots we get, the less capacity we'll have to dwell on the negative.

Think of it in terms of science. Newton's first law of motion states, "An object at rest stays at rest and an object in motion stays in motion." If we want to be productive, we have to get moving so we can keep moving. This means the way we begin our day is very important.

There are many things we can do to increase our productivity in the morning and put ourselves in the best position to capitalize on creating momentum for our day:

- Plan and prepare everything the night before;
- Stop hitting the snooze button on your alarm;
- Avoid beginning the day by reading emails;
- Start with small things to make immediate progress and begin moving forward; and
- Try to get as much done as you can in the morning to generate enough momentum to carry yourself through the rest of the day

A more productive life may begin with simply reframing your goals. Psychologist Peter Gollwitzer introduced the concept of implementation intentions in 1999. Studies conducted on implementation intentions have found that people who use them have an increased likelihood of successfully accomplishing their goals by up to 40 percent. Implementation intentions are setting a specific goal for behavior in response to a cue or event that will be encountered in the future.[3]

Implementation intentions can be formed by creating "if-then" statements. The "if" part of the statement is our cue or event; the "then" part of the statement is the response we plan to make when the cue or event occurs. This is a small plan we can put in place to overcome obstacles in the future, and the fact that it is so small just might "trick" our brains into making it work.

Here are a few examples: If your goal is to decrease the amount of time you spend on social media, then you might say, "If I want to read my Facebook messages, then I will set the timer for 20 minutes." If your goal is to eat less chocolate, then you might say, "If I get a craving for chocolate, then I will eat an apple."

Why are implementation intentions so successful?

- They eliminate our choices. When we have multiple choices that seem at odds with one another, they can become obstacles that keep us from focusing on our goals. With implementation intentions, we already have a plan in place.
- They make our responses automatic. You will have already made your decision about what you will do when a specific situation occurs, so you won't have to waste time trying to come up with a plan. You'll be less likely to be swayed by short-term temptations. When your response is automatic, you can keep your eye on the prize and just keep moving forward.
- They conserve our willpower. We discussed earlier that we may only have a certain amount of willpower and that the sooner we are able to create a positive

habit, the better. When we hand over our decisions to our implementation intentions, we can keep ourselves from getting tired and worn down by trying to keep up our self-control. We can conserve our willpower for when we really need it, and use it to help us achieve our goals.

If a more productive life is what you desire, then there are many small things you can do to take steps to make that happen. From tracking your time and activities to focusing on the positive and creating momentum, to reframing your goals into concrete small plans of action, a more productive you may be just around the corner. All you have to do is take the first step.

Key Habit Takeaway of This Chapter:

Track your tasks. Track how much time you spend on work. Track how much time you waste. Track your victories.

7

Practice Moderation

We are sometimes our own worst enemies. We tend to put a lot of pressure on ourselves and get frustrated when we feel like we aren't getting results as quickly as we think we should. Sometimes we just need to take a breath and slow down a bit. We can't take everything so seriously all the time. We often rush through life because we are afraid if we don't, we will miss out on something.

It's important to remember that change doesn't happen in an instant and no one (except maybe our impatient inner voice) expects us to accomplish all of our goals in life by tomorrow. We have to cut ourselves a little slack instead of expecting that we will instantly make a change, then being upset with ourselves for not meeting such an unrealistic expectation. We overestimate how much we can accomplish in a month and underestimate how much can change in a year.

We live in a time where instant gratification is valued, but remember that the most meaningful changes happen over time. It isn't a fast process at all. It can happen so slowly and steadily that we may not even be aware that the change is happening at all. There are times when it's only looking back years later that we can recognize all of the major changes that took place in our lives.

In school, we are taught that if we work hard to achieve certain goals (test scores), we are doing a great job, and if we don't, we are failing. It isn't until we have graduated that we realize that life doesn't always work that way.

While working toward goals is a good thing and it gives our life direction and meaning, we eventually come to find out that it is sometimes the journey on the way to a goal that teaches us a more valuable lesson than actually achieving the goal itself.

We learn that it is okay for our goals to change and evolve over time. Sometimes we discover that the goals we set for ourselves in the past no longer fit our present life view, and they are no longer something we really want for our lives. There is no shame in abandoning old goals and creating new ones as long as we are learning and growing. Sometimes the journey and what we take away from it is what matters.

If you talk to people who have had a great variety of life experiences, traveled all over the world, and have had the good fortune to meet people who come from all walks of life, they will tell you that people are very similar no matter where they live or what circumstances they have experienced.

Everyone spends a lot of their time concerned with food, money, their job, and their family. Everyone is interested in how others perceive them and are worried about projecting a good image to the world. Everyone is proud of where they come from. They have insecurities and fears that bother them. Everyone is afraid to fail or look stupid or incompetent to others. Everyone loves their family and friends dearly, even though those are the people who can also irritate them the most.

This seems to hold true regardless of culture, individual success, socioeconomic background, or social status. People are just people, and they have far more similarities with one another than differences.

It is often assumed that homeland, government, religion, and culture make people very different from each other. In reality, many of these differences are just superficial ones which were created accidentally by geography and history. The truth is humanity should unite us so much more than it divides us, because we are far more similar than we may suspect or even be comfortable with.

If we judge people by their actions rather than who we believe them to be, we may gain a far more accurate picture of the type of person they really are. There are all kinds of people in the world. We can't possibly know what kind of person we are really around unless we spend enough time with them to observe what they do, rather than making assumptions based on their appearance, gender, or where they are from.

In today's society, people seem to feel a strong sense of importance and uniqueness. They often feel that they are special and better than other people.

When we believe that our feelings and struggles are so unique that no one else can possibly understand the pain or hardships we've had to endure, we begin to feel superior to those around us. Instead of taking comfort in the similarities we all share and acknowledging we are not alone, we reject the notion that there is a shared human experience and cling to the feelings of entitlement and superiority, even if doing so leaves us feeling miserable and isolated.

Practicing a little moderation about our self-importance, our quality of life will go a long way towards improving. While we don't want to think negatively about ourselves and have a poor sense of self-worth, it isn't necessary to think the sun rises and sets on us, either. A middle-of-the-road approach to our feelings of self-importance and uniqueness will help us stay based in reality and will cause us a lot less stress and sadness in the long run. If we can

Practice Moderation

make practicing moderation a habit in our lives, we will become a lot happier.

Just quiet your mind and remind yourself that life is simple, there are good people out there, and not everyone is out to get you. Life doesn't have to be a competition. You are worthy as you are.

Moderation will serve you well in nearly every area of your life. When it comes to eating, people often blame their struggles on bad foods. Foods aren't necessarily bad if they are consumed in moderation. Eating a piece of chocolate, drinking a soda, or enjoying some French fries won't cause all of our struggles with obesity and other health problems unless they are eaten in excess and compounded by other problems like not exercising, a lack of sleep, and high stress.

While we want to limit our intake of less healthy foods as much as we can, we need to strike a balance that works for us. That may mean instead of cutting these temptations out of our lives completely, we only get to eat them once a week or on a special occasion. We need to take a look at our goals and ask ourselves if we are trying to lose weight or trying to live a healthier life. Then we can find our moderation and the right balance for us.

Moderation in our diets is all about eating a variety of healthy foods and only adding the less healthy foods on occasion and with portion control.

Habits of the Disciplined

A good saying to incorporate into your life is, "Eat to live; don't live to eat." This means food can't be given such a high priority in our lives if we truly want to have a healthy lifestyle.

When you sit down to eat a meal, try to turn your focus to your family and friends. Enjoy your time together and have good conversations so that you are not overly attentive to your food. Try not to watch television or pay attention to your phone or computer during a meal, because then you may engage in mindless eating and not even realize when you feel full.

Practicing the habit of moderation when it comes to sleep is beneficial, as getting too much or too little sleep can be harmful to your health.

Moderation in the workplace comes from having a plan and being willing to stick with it. It is important to find a good work-life balance.

When creating your plan, you need to take into account where your stressors are coming from. Are you feeling guilty that you aren't able to spend enough quality time with your spouse or children? Are you stressed that you won't be able to provide for your family? Are you worried about maintaining the lavish lifestyle to which you have become accustomed, or are you worried that you can never earn enough?

When you know where your fears and concerns are

coming from, you can begin to create a plan that will help you address those concerns and begin to find moderation and balance in your life.

Keep in mind your personal and financial goals as you form your plan. Having goals and a sense of purpose and direction can help you stay motivated and focused on moving forward, even when obstacles and setbacks occur.

If you don't strive to find that balance and moderation and you aren't able to make a plan to address your personal and financial goals, you may find that stress will begin to take over. When you are under increased stress, you may start to experience frequent headaches or migraines, experience a spike in your blood pressure, feel pain in your chest, be more susceptible to contagious ailments such as colds or the flu as your immune system struggles to keep your resistance up, and in severe instances, stress can even lead to a stroke or heart attack.

When it comes to setting priorities and finding a balance in your work, domestic, and financial goals, understand that it is important to save money and invest for the future, but it is also important to find ways to enjoy the present. Living well in the present while still planning for the future are both important and vital to living a balanced life, as well as forming the habit of moderation.

At the risk of sounding like my mother, I will stress: "Everything in moderation." That is how we can strike a balance in our lives, and it is a crucial habit to add to our repertoire if we want to have a healthy lifestyle.

> **Key Habit Takeaway of This Chapter:**
>
> Practice moderation in every area of life.

8

Forget Multi-Tasking

Multi-tasking is one of the biggest myths I have encountered in my adult life. No one really does it well. In fact, no one does it. There is no such thing as multi-tasking, just a quick shift of focus between activities. But by splitting your focus, you won't perform at your best in any area.

Multi-tasking is really the unconscious practice of repeatedly distracting yourself. The Human-Computer Interaction Institute at Carnegie Mellon University found through their research that it can take up to 25 minutes to regain our focus after we get distracted. While multi-tasking makes you think that you are getting more done in less time, in reality, you are not.[1]

Attention residue is an effect which was identified in 2009 by the author Sophie Leroy in her paper "Why Is It so Hard to Do My Work?" Leroy notes that in the modern office environment, employees often have to transition back and forth between projects they are currently working on. She found that when people moved from one task to another, their attention didn't instantly follow. A residue of their attention was still stuck thinking about the original task.[2]

The results from her experiment demonstrated that people who experience attention residue after they move to a new task will likely not perform as well on that task. She found that those employees spend most of their time switching tasks and trying to get caught back up to where they were when they last left off instead of being able to keep moving forward. It becomes kind of a cycle of taking one step forward and two steps back every time they attempt to multi-task.

Stanford researcher Clifford Nass also studied the work patterns displayed by multi-taskers. The researchers divided their subjects into groups according to those who regularly performed media multi-tasking and those who did not.

In the first test, the groups were shown images of colored rectangles, and after the image was flashed twice, they had to determine if the rectangles had changed positions from one frame to the next. They were all told to ignore the blue rectangles. The people who were not typically multi-taskers could do that easily, but those who regularly try to multi-task couldn't ignore the irrelevant images and performed poorly on the task. The researchers predicted that since the multi-taskers couldn't ignore things easily, perhaps they had better memories.[3]

The second test they conducted proved that prediction incorrect. The subjects were shown sequences of letters of the alphabet and were asked to identify the letters that made a repeat appearance. Once again, those who did not engage in multi-tasking outperformed their multi-tasking peers.

It seems people who multi-task are not able to filter out irrelevant information in order to focus on the goal at hand, and all of the irrelevant information slows down their progress.

Hungarian psychologist Mihaly Csikszentmihalyi believes that the best possible working mode we can hope to achieve is flow, and it is only possible to achieve flow when you don't multi-task. He identifies eight characteristics of flow:

- Being completely focused on the task at hand;
- Having clear goals complete with a reward and feedback;
- Being able to speed up or slow down time;
- What you experience is its own intrinsic reward;
- The challenge the task poses and the skills required are balanced;
- Actions and awareness are intertwined; and
- Feeling control over the task at hand

Flow is reached through focus, not multi-tasking. If you can enjoy yourself and challenge yourself just enough that you can still feel at ease, you will find that you are "in the zone" and making real progress.[4]

For example, think of a sports team preparing to face a rival. They need to be able to focus on the task ahead of them and tune out distractions.

They should be able to identify a clear goal as a team and know the reward they are trying to earn. The team needs to feel that they have an adequate amount of time to prepare without dwelling on negativity or stress.

Playing in the rivalry game is a reward in its own right. It is important for the team to feel that they are on a level playing field with their rivals and that they have the skills they need to be successful. They are aware of the game plan and everyone on the team is aware of the contributions they need to make to it.

Finally, the team needs to feel like they have some control over the outcome of the game. If they can accomplish all of those things, then they have reached flow, and they have a greater likelihood of achieving their desired outcome of winning the game.

Cal Newport identified the concept of "deep work." Newport classifies deep work as "professional activities performed in a state of distraction-free concentration that push your cognitive capabilities to their limits."[5]

Don't mistake deep work as being a tedious endeavor. It is entirely possible for it to be enjoyable, challenging, and creative all at once. It takes practice to be able to work deeply for long stretches of time.

Newport believes you should work at a high level with intense intervals which increase over time to give you your desired outcome of getting a lot of quality work accomplished. He suggests being focused and on-task for at least 90 minutes, then practicing until you can increase that amount of time to 2-4 hours or more.

Tracking your time by marking tallies of how many hours you spend working or when you meet some of your goals may help you to incorporate deep work into your schedule, and scheduling deep work time a few weeks in advance may prove helpful as well.

I find that if I am able to block out some time and mark it on the calendar in advance, I am more likely to be able to keep my professional time sacred. I don't let other things interrupt my work, and I can be free of distractions. Then I can truly dive more deeply into my writing and stay focused for a longer stretch of time, which means I am able to accomplish more. Deep work makes me a more efficient writer.

No matter what you call it—flow, deep work, or simply avoiding multi-tasking—when we are able to block out distractions and focus solely on our goals and the task in front of us, we are able to be more productive and accomplish more. I can't think of anyone who wouldn't want that.

> **Key Habit Takeaway of This Chapter:**
>
> Be the ultimate mono-tasker. Multi-tasking weakens your focus and you'll end up performing poorly or in a mediocre manner.

9

Happiness Boosters

The whole nature of human survival involves us seeking pleasure and avoiding pain. Our brain gets in on the act too, housing neurochemicals which are linked to happiness. We need to be conscious of the ways to unlock them to take advantage of the benefits they have to offer.[1]

Typically, these neurochemicals have been triggered in part by physical activity. In this modern digital age, as we become less physically active these neurochemicals can easily get ignored. This is why it's so crucial to make new habits which will assist in the production of these neurochemicals rather than relying on supplementary pills to boost our happiness. Let's take a closer look at some of these neurochemicals and how are they linked to our happiness.

Dopamine

Dopamine is the neurochemical that is released when we set a goal and achieve it; it's connected to reward, motivation, memory, attention, and body movement regulation. It is the pleasure we feel when we receive a reward.

Dopamine creates feelings of pleasure and reward, which drives us to repeat a specific behavior and thus work toward our goals. Dopamine helps us to make plans and have the willpower to resist obstacles and impulsive choices which may stand in the way of us meeting our goals.

There are many simple, healthy choices we can make to help boost our dopamine levels. Many foods can help increase these levels: almonds, apples, avocados, bananas, beets, chocolate, meats, green, leafy vegetables, and foods high in protein are just a few excellent sources of dopamine.

It is also helpful to avoid eating foods which may deplete the amount of dopamine in our brains. Foods high in saturated fats, sugar, caffeine, or that use artificial sweeteners should be eaten in very small amounts if increasing dopamine levels is the goal.

There are healthy lifestyle choices you can make which will also support dopamine production. Getting plenty of physical exercise, even low- or no-impact exercises like walking or doing yoga, is one of the most beneficial things you can do to keep your brain sharp and increase your dopamine levels. It is even better if you can exercise while enjoying time in the sun, as sunlight has also been proven to aid in the production of dopamine.

Practicing meditation is another way you can increases dopamine and improve your ability to concentrate. Setting a regular routine and schedule to help ensure that you get an adequate amount of rest and keep stressors at a minimum is so beneficial to not only your dopamine production, but also your overall health.[2]

Endorphins

Endorphins, the brain's "feel-good" chemicals, are another type of neurochemical that can serve to give our happiness a boost. Endorphins are produced by the pituitary gland and the hypothalamus. Production increases when you participate in strenuous physical exercise and sexual intercourse. Endorphins make you feel less pain and fewer negative effects from stress. Endorphins can give you a feeling of euphoria and improve the strength of your immune system.

Things we can do to increase our endorphin production include eating chocolate or chili peppers and participating in physical exercise. Acupuncture and practicing meditation are additional ways we can help raise the levels of endorphins in our brains.[3]

Some aromas and scents can influence the release of endorphins. For example, the scent of lavender and vanilla can aid in releasing endorphins, thus reducing anxiety. Try adding a few drops of natural vanilla extract to your morning coffee or tea, have a relaxing bath with some lavender-scented candles, or add the essential oil version of these scents to your bathwater. It works magic and studies have proven that you can have better sleep if you take a lavender- or vanilla-scented bath in the evening.

Serotonin

Serotonin is believed to act as a mood stabilizer. It is the neurochemical that increases our feelings of worthiness and sense of belonging; when our serotonin levels are high, we feel good. It helps to improve our self-esteem and makes us feel more confident.

One way to increase your serotonin levels is via supplements that contain the amino acid tryptophan. Serotonin is synthesized from tryptophan. However, we may get the same benefits naturally, by consuming food that is high in tryptophan. High-protein foods like eggs, cheese, pineapples, tofu, salmon, nuts and seeds, and turkey meat are rich in tryptophan. Add them to your diet.

Remember that high-tryptophan foods won't increase your serotonin level by themselves. There's one special element to add to this diet: carbs. Carbs help your body to release more insulin, which aids amino acid absorption and leaves tryptophan in the blood. So mix your high-tryptophan foods with some healthy carbs, and increase your chances to have a serotonin boost.[4]

Another thing you can do to increase your levels of serotonin is to challenge yourself and give yourself a purpose to work toward. Exercise, exposure to bright light, and the aforementioned diet enhanced by foods high in tryptophan are all ways to gain a boost in mood from serotonin.[5]

Oxytocin

Oxytocin, also called the "love molecule", is a neurochemical, which can help boost our happiness and life satisfaction. It strengthens our bonds with other people and provides us with strong feelings of loyalty and trust.

In today's world it is easy to feel isolated as we often spend less time communicating with others face-to-face than we have in the past. In order to counteract the effects of the unhealthy solitude and increase our levels of oxytocin, we can become more involved in our communities, or even work out with a buddy or in an exercise class at the gym. The more time we spend with people in person, the better.

Spending time with others, however, is not always possible. Some studies have concluded it is possible to get a similar boost in oxytocin by holding our pets. The bond between humans and their animals is often very strong.[6]

Until recently, it was thought that oxytocin only served to magnify positive social experiences. New studies have revealed that it can also magnify negative social experiences.

In 2013, researchers at Northwestern Medicine were among the first to study the darker side of oxytocin. Their research found that during and after an experience of social setback or trauma, oxytocin focused on a part of the brain that strengthened memories based on fear. While oxytocin can make us feel more connected and safe, it can also increase feelings of loneliness and sadness. It seems that when we feel stress in social situations, the parts of the brain that use oxytocin may change.

Be mindful of the power of oxytocin and focus on releasing it due to pleasant social interactions. For example, hug others as often as you can. Eight hugs a day keeps anxiety away. Give gifts, share your food with others, help other people, practice loving kindness, meditation, express your love to people, and pet animals. Generally speaking, practice acts of kindness towards yourself and others.

GABA

GABA is the main inhibitory neurotransmitter in the brain. It balances our neurons from over-firing and being overstimulated. Increasing our GABA neurochemicals could help with stress, anxiety, muscle tension, convulsions, insomnia, and relaxation.

Practicing meditation and yoga seems to be among the best things you can do to increase your GABA production.

A study published in *The Journal of Alternative and Complementary Medicine* separated the participants into two groups: those who would read for 60 minutes and those who would do yoga for 60 minutes. The study found that the participants who did yoga for an hour had a 27 percent increase in GABA levels as opposed to those who read a book.[7]

There are not a lot of other healthy lifestyle changes offered as possible boosts to GABA production. Anyone who has a serious deficiency in GABA should consult their doctor for what possible treatment options may be the best for them.

Some natural supplements can also increase your GABA release. Consult with your doctor before you decide to consume any. Magnolia officinalis, also known as magnolia bark, for example, has been widely used in traditional Chinese medicine as its active ingredients include honokiol and magnolol, which are found in the bark of the tree. Honokiol and magnolol act as positive allosteric modulators of GABA receptors and help with the symptoms of anxiety, depression, and seizures by promoting relaxation.[8]

While our brains are hardwired to encourage us to seek pleasure and avoid pain, sometimes just leaving them to their own devices is not enough. If we want to unlock our neurochemicals so we can take advantage of all they have to offer, there are things we can do that will help our brains increase the production of these happiness boosters.

Practicing meditation and yoga, eating healthy, nutrient-rich foods, exercising regularly, spending time in the sun, setting goals and working to achieve them, and spending more time with people face to face are all lifestyle choices we can make that can improve our health, happiness, and overall well-being.

Key Habit Takeaway of This Chapter:

Eat healthy food and do activities that aid the release of good neurochemicals in your body.

10

Success Habits

Name five skills you have. That may not be as easy as you think. But if you were asked the same question about a family member, friend, or mentor, you probably would find it much easier to answer. It turns out that honest, positive, thought-provoking self-analysis can be a more daunting task than you might expect. Gaining a deeper understanding of yourself is critical to success. Let's get started!

When you try to identify what skills you are proficient in, start by asking yourself some questions.

- What do you like to do?
- What are you passionate about?
- What do you find yourself wanting to work on more often?
- What comes easily to you that others find difficult?
- What do you consider to be your biggest accomplishments?

Answering these questions will help you get to know your wants better and will go a long way toward helping you uncover your strongest skill set.

There is a difference between skills and "motivated skills." Skills are talents that you have, but you may or may not like to use them. For example, I know I have a strong ability to be persuasive when I speak with others. That is a skill of mine. However, I often don't care to use the skill because as an author and a teacher, I prefer to present people with facts in an unbiased way and encourage them to draw their own conclusions and think for themselves.

"Motivated skills" are the skills that you have and enjoy using. For example, I know I have a talent for preparing healthy recipes that even picky eaters will eat. That is also something I enjoy doing. I don't need to be convinced to cook for others. I like to do it, and I am happy to cook for family and friends every chance I get.

To identify your "motivated skills," start by brainstorming a list of goals you have achieved, accomplishments you are particularly proud of, and experiences you enjoyed over the past two to five years. They may be work-related or personal.

Rank the items on your list and identify the one you think is the best. Then write on your list what you did, how you did it, and what happened. This will reveal your skills and make it abundantly clear where your talents and passions lie.

Author Mark Manson writes about three life skills he thinks are critically important for everyone to have, but that no one was ever taught.

The first key life skill—or habit if you like—is how to stop taking everything personally.

We all have a tendency to make things about us even when they really aren't. We like to take all of the credit for making good things happen and then turn ourselves into a victim when something bad happens. Pain and sadness are things that happen to everyone, and we would be better served to remember that sometimes things just happen and they really have nothing to do with us personally.

The second life skill Manson identifies as being critically important is how to be persuaded and change your mind.

Sometimes people hold onto their beliefs at all costs and make them a part of their identity. When this happens, often despite overwhelming evidence that contradicts their opinion, people will refuse to change their mind and will still wholeheartedly defend their beliefs. We would have a far better society if people were willing to at least listen to the other side's point of view and entertain the possibility that their own beliefs might be wrong and need to evolve.

The third key life skill is being able to act without knowing what the result will be.

From the time we are young, we are taught to do something and expect a certain result. For example, children do their homework and study for tests because they expect it will result in them earning a good grade and they want to please their parents and teachers. Adults do their jobs because they know it will result in them earning a paycheck.[1]

The problem occurs when we have to make decisions without knowing the result we can expect in advance. We may feel paralyzed or afraid to do anything at all because we worry that we will make the wrong choice.

Manson suggests that we start with small decisions to practice this skill, and then when the big consequential decisions come up, we will feel better prepared to handle them. It's important to be willing to fail at times because this is the way to experience great success. Embrace change and grow with it.

If we want to create habits for success, we need goals. Without goals, we are missing the directions that tell us where we want to go and the focus that will keep us on track and moving forward until we get there. When we set goals, we are taking control of the direction of our life. Thankfully, goals also come with built-in checkpoints that will let us know if we are really succeeding because they define what success should look like to us.

It is helpful to keep several things in mind when we set goals. First, the goal should be one that you really care about and have the motivation, drive, and a sense of urgency to achieve.

The goal needs to be S.M.A.R.T.:

- **S**pecific: Clearly defined.
- **M**easurable: You should know exactly what it will look like to you if you are successful.
- **A**ttainable: Challenging, but not impossible to reach.
- **R**elevant: Aligned with the vision and direction you want for your life.
- **T**ime Bound: Goals need a deadline to help you stay on track and create a sense of urgency for you.

Set written goals. Writing it down makes the goal more real and important in your mind. The goal should also come with its own to-do list that acts as your plan for the steps you need to accomplish before your goal can be achieved. Finally, you need to keep checking in on your progress toward your goal and make revisions to the goal or plan, if necessary. That will help you see it through, even when obstacles get in your way.

Keep in mind that your goals are a work in progress, and as you grow and change, your goal may very well need to evolve right along with you.

Goals don't need to be set in stone. In fact, they should be just the opposite: flexible and serving as a guideline for you. The plan that you set on day one may look very different from the plan that you actually follow to achieve your goal, and there is absolutely nothing wrong with that.

As we discussed earlier, having a purpose by setting a goal is key to creating a habit for success. However, the path we take toward achieving that goal, and perhaps even the goal itself, should be ready and able to change as new and unexpected things pop up along the way.

Another key component to creating habits for success is to commit yourself to being a lifelong learner. As a teacher who believes wholeheartedly that knowledge is power and we should never stop learning, this, to me, is one of the most critical elements to creating habits for success.

In the field of education, it seems like the concept of lifelong learning has been around forever, but in fact, it stemmed from the phrase "lifelong learners," which was created by Leslie Watkins in 1993. Lifelong learning means that learning isn't only for children, and it doesn't only take place in the classroom. In our complex and fast-paced digital world, it is simply detrimental to think that once you have earned your degree, you can sit back and not have to learn anymore. If this is your worldview, don't be surprised to wake up one day to find that the world continued to grow and change without you and has now passed you by.

Lifelong learning needs to be about learning to know, learning to do, learning to coexist, and learning to be.

Learning to know means that we should be far more concerned with learning the tools available to help us in our quest to educate ourselves and achieve our goals (learning how to learn instead of what to learn) than we are with learning a certain piece of information. Chances are that information may become obsolete as new facts are discovered. It is impossible for us to know all of the information we will need in our lives, but we can certainly learn how and where to find information when we need it.

Learning to do means we need to focus on not only learning skills that we will need today, but also on learning skills and talents that will be important in the future. We need the ability to adapt and evolve as our world does.

Learning to coexist means we need to be able to appreciate and embrace the strengths that living and working in a diverse society has to offer. We need to learn how to positively resolve conflicts that may arise and be willing to listen to viewpoints that may differ from our own.

Learning to be involves educating the whole person rather than only the mind. It includes making ourselves better-rounded and finding balance in all of the different areas of our lives.

Lifelong learners continue to educate themselves because they are self-motivated to better themselves and to learn and grow, not because someone is requiring them to do so.[2]

The key to a healthy and balanced life is education. When lifelong learners educate themselves, they are helping their brains at the same time. Using their brains to constantly learn new things protects their brain cells from atrophy. Brain plasticity creates a positive cycle: The more people interact and work with the new knowledge they gain, the more connections their brains will make, and the stronger the connections become. In turn, the more they use their newly gained knowledge, the faster they will make what they learned a permanent addition to their lives.

Your brain keeps everything running in your life. It is important that you keep it "tuned up" and healthy so it can be at its peak level of performance. Take good care of your brain by learning how to train your brain.

Neuroplasticity is a scientific term which began to gain more attention and support in the latter half of the 20th century. It refers to the lasting changes that the brain is able to make over a person's lifetime. Prior to the fairly recent research, scientists believed that neurogenesis didn't exist. It was widely believed the brain developed rapidly up to a certain point in early childhood and then it stayed mainly unchanged for the remainder of a person's life.

Neuroplasticity has now disproven that theory. People can continue to learn while the brain changes and evolves well into adulthood.

How does neuroplasticity work? Neuroplasticity is the brain's ability to reorganize and change itself as it takes in new information over time and decides whether the new information should become permanent within our minds.

It helps to make the brain resilient as it tries to heal from injuries or mental ailments and disorders like a stroke, depression, learning disabilities, or ADHD.[3]

The brain is more likely to change when it is ready for it by being attentive and motivated so that it may release neurochemicals allowing the change to happen. What changes in the brain are the connections between neurons that strengthen over time.

The changes in the brain only become permanent if the brain thinks they are new enough and important enough to become lasting changes. Neuroplasticity does not only allow positive changes in the brain; negative changes can occur as well.

It is important that as adults and lifelong learners, we are open to accept growth and change in all areas of our lives. When it comes to relationships, it is all about learning from past mistakes, figuring out what caused an argument, correctly interpreting body language, listening to others' feelings better, and becoming more aware of what is occurring in the present, as well as what happened in the past.

Lifelong learners are encouraged to develop skills that are rare and valuable to others and to do something that is good and helpful to others, says Cal Newport in his book *So Good They Can't Ignore You*. People who love their jobs have certain things in common. They have a lot of control in the workplace and are financially stable because they have found their rare and valuable skills that are in demand and that employers are willing to pay for. They have found a meaningful mission and purpose to their careers. Instead of switching careers to try to follow a passion, it is better to choose something that you can master as you continue to improve your craft through lifelong learning.

We have no way of knowing exactly what the future will hold for us, so how do we prepare for the careers of the future when we don't know what they will be? One thing is for sure—technology will play a big role in careers of the future. Some careers we have today will be completely automated a few decades from now.

Perhaps the most useful skill we will need in the future is autodidacticism. It is a Greek word which means "self-teaching." Being a lifelong learner will be even more important in the future than it is today. But what should people try to teach themselves that will be necessary skills in the future?

So far, computers haven't been able to copy our creativity, critical thinking, or ability to quickly and accurately make connections. Being a lifelong learner is going to be a vital skill.

Our educational system is still run on models from the 1950s and is not able to help us learn as quickly and efficiently as we need to in order to meet the demands of today's world, let alone the demands the future will bring. We are going to need to increase the speed at which we learn new things. We will have to be able to read and research information quickly in order to have any hope of keeping up with the pace of our rapidly changing world.

Mastering habits—being able to shed the bad ones while turning the healthy ones into lasting occupants in our lives—is something we should aspire to do.

Letting go of unrealistic expectations while still setting goals to improve our lives is critical if we want to enhance our lives with healthy habits. Without self-discipline our habits and dreams are little more than wishes, and we are no closer to achieving them.

Productivity is often an area people want to improve in their lives, and there are steps that can be taken to increase it. From tracking your time and activities to focusing on the positive and creating momentum, to reframing your goals into concrete small plans of action, a more productive you may be just around the corner.

Practicing meditation and yoga, eating healthy, nutrient-rich foods, exercising regularly, spending time in the sun, setting goals and working to achieve them, spending more time with people face to face, and committing ourselves to being lifelong learners are all lifestyle choices we can make that can improve our health, habits, happiness, and overall well-being.

It is tempting to want to make drastic changes in our lives and to try to change multiple things at once. However, it is important that we don't try to adopt a few new habits at the same time. If we try to change everything about our lives at once, we will be overwhelmed and stressed out and end up not changing anything at all.

Everything has to be conducted in moderation and balance, even change. We have to be patient and understand that meaningful change takes time. If we take the time to understand ourselves and make a commitment to putting the work in every day to try to improve ourselves and reach our goals, there is nothing that will prevent us from creating the life and habits we desire.

> **Key Habit Takeaway of This Chapter:**
>
> Know your strengths. Identify your "motivated skills." Set clear, achievable goals. Never stop learning.

11

Habits of a Good Life

Get familiar with your "whys" when you want to change a habit. Ask yourself why you want to be more productive. Is it to finish more tasks, to make more money, or to spend it on things that give you pleasure?

Why do you want to be a habitually nonviolent communicator? It is to avoid misunderstandings, the pain of social awkwardness, shunning, or being seen as argumentative. Those things can seriously hinder you in the workplace and in dating. I often hear people say they don't like confrontation and I personally believe it's because we don't teach people how to have productive and meaningful confrontation and arguments. It's so much about "I am right and you are wrong" vs. "this is my point and why I believe this way. Let's just agree to disagree. You're still my friend."

Since most of our day is composed by habitual activities,

it isn't hard to see how big of an impact a few good habits can make. Some habits have larger impacts than others. In this chapter I will talk about those little cognitive habits, which if adopted, can significantly reduce pain in your life and enhance pleasure.

Good habits, like patience, discipline, and acceptance, will take care of your goals automatically. For example, instead of focusing on your goal of losing thirty pounds, focus on developing healthy eating and fitness habits. The consistency and familiarity of good habits will keep you on track better than just simply have a goal. The initial willpower you feel when you set the goal will be depleted after a few weeks of starving. Eating genuinely healthy on the other hand would not starve you and would not include the stress factor of an overly strict diet that you could never imagine maintaining for the rest of your days.

What are those little cognitive habits that can have a large impact on every area of your life?

1) The "Something for Something" Principle

My father was very strict with my two brothers and me. Having two children of my own, today, I don't wonder why. One of his golden principles to instill in us was a strong work ethic from an early age in order to make us understand the value of… everything. He used to say that whenever you do or don't do something, it will cost you something else. What he meant was that in life, everything is a trade off. Everything has an opportunity cost.

Our day-to-day living is a series of tradeoffs. Whatever we want to do or achieve will cost us something else; marrying Simone cost me the ability to marry any of the other ladies queuing for the honor. Just kidding, I'm the luckiest man on Earth. But having a healthy marriage and being a devoted father has lots of opportunity costs. For example, I could never chase career paths that would demand I stay away from home for too long. I wanted to see my kids grow up and be there for them, not only see them when they are sleeping, tucked tight in bed. You don't get a six-figure salary without putting in time and focus, but you don't get a happy family without being present and empathetically listening to their problems, needs, and being there for them unconditionally.

Our time and energy is limited. This is why it's so crucial to know exactly what you want. What are the main values in your life? There are no wrong or right answers here, just be honest with yourself. Don't forget to check up on your values occasionally. We change and so do our priorities. Be aware when they do so you don't pay the opportunity cost of something irrelevant for too long.

How can you discover what your real values are? First and foremost, the right question isn't "What do I want?"

but rather "What am I willing to pay the highest tradeoff price for?"

Make it a habit to be mentally comfortable with the tradeoff for your choices. There will always be chances missed. Make sure to choose as wisely as possible, and then simply enjoy it. Don't waste your life on "what ifs" and mourning missed opportunities.

2) Focus On Fewer Things, but Do Them Better

Whenever I approach this subject my daughter tells me I think like an old man, but I must assume the risk and say it anyway. In our modern world everything is about chasing "more": more money, more skinny, more romances, more likes, more, more, more… One of the negative impacts of a world with seemingly endless opportunities, is that we can't have more of everything—opportunity cost, remember?

The best we can hope for with a "more" mentality is to act only on an average amount of opportunities. Why try to have everything and settle for guaranteed disappointment?

Rather, choose only a few things and do them well. You may not become the world champion in any of the things you choose, but at least you'll be the best version of yourself in them. Again, since your time and energy is limited, you can only focus on a couple of things very effectively. Choose these things wisely and let them give meaning to your life.

3) Don't Try So Hard

I know this sounds quite the opposite of what you always hear about trying. People get advice and encouragement to do their best, but they tend to confuse their best with "too much." Just think back to a time when you tried too hard to make friends, do better at your job, or be happy. People considered you over eager and disingenuous and subsequently avoided you. Trying too hard at your workplace can make you seem like a bootlicker or a brown-noser. Trying too hard to be happy will make you feel even more miserable.

What can you do? Where is the thin line between doing your best and trying too hard? As unhelpful as it may sound, your best already lies in front of you, or better phrased, within you. Take a little break, look around, and look inside your soul. Be grateful for whatever you have and whoever you are. Make it a habit to keep this gratitude alive in your heart while you simultaneously work your way toward what you desire. Just because you want to improve doesn't mean you are broken, wrong, or unlovable.

Stop to appreciate the little joys in life. If you can't enjoy what you have now, you probably won't enjoy that bigger something you're trying so hard to achieve either.

4) The Pareto Principle of Your Life

The Pareto principle states that 80 percent of the output will come from 20 percent of the input. In other words, 80 percent of the results of something are generated by 20 percent of the actions taken. We could also interpret it as the rule of 4:1. In business, 20 percent of customers often generate 80 percent of sales. In time management, 20 percent of the time invested gets 80 percent of the job done.

What if we applied this same rule to our lives?

- What 20 percent of your activities do you enjoy the most?
- Who are the 20 percent of your friends you spend 80 percent of your time with?
- What are the 20 percent of things that cause sorrow in 80 percent of your life?
- What 20 percent pairs of your shoes do you wear 80 percent of the time?

Once you answer these or similar questions, it will be much easier to know where to focus your energies to get the most out of your life. This also applies to the negatives. For example, the 20 percent of things that make up 80 percent of your time-wasting (video games, TV, playing on your smartphone) can be easily identified and trashed—yes trashed—with this observation. You can turn the ratios around: which activities eat up 80 percent of your time, but only bring you 20 percent of your happiness?

When I started using the Pareto principle in my life, it first helped me with my finances. I realized that 80 percent of the things I spent my money on didn't make me happy. This realization triggered me to change my shopping habits, buy more healthy food, and spend more on experiences with my family versus fishing stuff and constant garage improvement gadgets.

You can apply the Pareto principle in your relationships too. What are the 20 percent of bad habits that cause 80 percent of your arguments? What are the 20 percent of activities that create 80 percent of the loving feelings in your relationship?

We can create efficiency in so many areas of life by simply adopting the habit of Pareto principle analysis into our lives.

Key Habit Takeaway of This Chapter:

Accept that everything in life is a tradeoff. Focus on fewer things and do them better. Don't try so hard. Use the Pareto principle in your personal life.

12

The Stoic Way to a Good Life

What Is the Core Value of Your Life?

No, seriously. If you don't know the answer, please take the time and think about it now. Do you cherish your family the most? Your job? Do you worship money? Fame? This is a judgment-free zone. There are no right or wrong answers. What matters is that you are honest with yourself.

Why am I even asking this question? What do your values have to do with habits?

Quite a bit, in fact. The last good habit to acquire that I cover in this book is expressing gratitude and controlling insatiability.

According to stoics, we're unlikely to have a happy and meaningful life if we don't overcome our insatiability. And when it comes to happiness, we'll be happiest when we learn to find joy in what we have and in what comes from within.

Our unhappiness is rooted in our insatiable nature. We make our happiness dependent to some external, worldly good—let's say a promotion. We start working hard to achieve this goal, but when we get it, we instantly lose interest.

On one hand, we get shocked that the goal didn't deliver the expected happiness, while on the other hand, we're still greedy. "Oh, this goal wasn't big enough. That's why it doesn't make me happy." So we dig further. We want something else instead, something even bigger.

I don't mean we shouldn't aim for more or strive to become better. We should. But we shouldn't run from one goal to another without truly appreciating what we have, or stopping for a moment to say, "Thank you, dear Lord, for letting this happen. For giving me the strength and wisdom to accomplish this goal. I am truly grateful for being here and now, having what I have."

If you are not religious, no problem. Find your own way of expressing gratitude. Learn to take a break to appreciate what you have, rather than continuously trying to catch the future.

> *"The easiest and best way to achieve happiness is to want the things you already have."*
>
> —William Irvine

In *A Guide to the Good Life: The Ancient Art of Stoic Joy*, William Irvine describes the most important values stoicism teaches us. Following Cato's, Seneca's, and Marcus Aurelius's works, Irvine created a comprehensive book about stoicism. To complement the information you read in this chapter, I recommend you read his book. If you are more interested in stoicism, read the aforementioned ancient geniuses' works also. There is a lot to learn from these works, even if you don't agree with the stoics.

One of the core values of stoic philosophy is self-discipline. Having control over your thoughts, and thus your actions, can help you determine what you want to do with your life. If you have a lack of self-discipline, you'll have to walk a path determined by someone else. I talked about the importance of self-discipline and how to adopt good habits in relation to it earlier in this book.

Tranquility is another state highly appraised by the stoics. It is a psychological state in which people experience negative emotions like grief, anxiety, and fear, but also positive emotions like joy. According to Seneca, you have to learn to use your reasoning ability to get rid of all that intrigues or scares you. Accept that the world is bipolar—good and bad coexist. If you expect only good, your life will be stressful and you'll never feel truly safe. The more you can accept the bipolar nature of the world, the more tranquility and freedom you'll have in your life.

Practice Poverty

Human nature tends to lead us into taking what we have for granted—our jobs, our smartphones, our bank accounts, even the air we breathe and the health we have. Stoics encourage us to change this bad habit by thinking about and practicing poverty.

Start thinking about losing everything you take for granted. Imagine losing your health, including your ability to speak, walk, and swallow. Picture a world where your family or your wealth or your freedom would disappear. How would you feel if you lost your ability to speak, hear, walk, breathe, and swallow? How would you feel if you lost your freedom?

Can you feel that lump in your throat? Don't get me wrong, I don't mean to make you feel depressed or anxious. This practice is not about making you constantly stressed about what will happen next. The point is to prepare you. We feel safe because in most seconds of our lives, nothing bad happens. But then there comes that one second when it does.

Almost 40 years have passed since my father died in front of my eyes. One moment he was playing with my brother and me, the next moment he grabbed his chest, fell on the ground, and never got up again. He was younger than I am now. Nothing like that's happened in my life since then. There was just that one horrible second out of the million normal ones. And that one second was enough for me to lose my father.

This is not negative thinking, but a sure way to enhance our feelings of gratitude toward what we have now. Whatever you have in this very moment are your riches. There is no value in future expectations or past grumblings. You have zero influence on both. Think about what you have now and how very little you do to cherish it.

Take time—right now—and give thanks for five things you have in the present moment. From your half-full Nutella jar to your faithful wife; anything will do.

But how do you practice poverty?

If you allow too many pleasures in your life and try to live as comfortably as possible 24/7, nothing will seem bearable when a crisis comes. This is not because that crisis is too much to bear, but because you became soft during the sunny period. Make sure you don't get too comfortable. This way you'll be able to appreciate comfort better and be happier when you get it.

If you expose yourself to self-chosen discomfort from time to time, you'll be more able to handle hard times that bring true discomfort. You may also have a larger comfort zone during unpredictable or bad events.

Exposing yourself to discomfort includes dealing with annoying people. When someone's behavior upsets you, reflect for a few minutes on your own shortcomings. By recognizing others' mistakes in yourself, you will become more empathetic to others. You will realize that often what you find annoying about others may be something you do too. What upsets people is not the facts themselves, but their judgments on these facts.

One of the most worshipped concepts of the 21st century is fame, and people often pursue it. Everybody has different reasons for wanting it and aspirations for their desired level of fame. Some want worldwide fame, some only regional or workplace popularity, but almost everyone seeks the admiration of others. But the price of fame, more often than not, is so great that it exceeds any benefits.

So if you consider seeking fame, know that it is a fickle companion. Fame is like the consumerist society—it stays only until you make your first mistake. Then it shows up somewhere else.

Try to be indifferent to what people think of you—not only regarding their disapproval, but also their approval. Cato consciously did or said things to trigger the contempt of others only so he could practice ignoring it.

A stoic philosophy seems difficult to adopt in our money- and status-oriented world. However, if you learn to simplify your life just a little based on these ancient wisdoms, you'll become much more fulfilled. As a stoic habit, introduce days of low modern stimuli, days of practicing poverty, and everyday gratitude.

For example, decide that every Saturday you'll disconnect from the world and that you'll try to live as people lived before television, Internet, or telephones were invented. To practice poverty, have a set of very cheap and low-quality clothes and consciously wear them one day a month while you eat cheap food and only drink water. Try going into the cold underdressed, or into the rain without an umbrella or raincoat.

Learn to value the things you have. And to be able to truly value them, you have to experience what it would be like to lose them. Of course, don't lose them for real; just take a few moments and imagine how it would feel if you did.

Key Habit Takeaway of This Chapter:

Be grateful. Don't take your good luck or your life for granted. Practice poverty.

Final Words

Now take a few deep breaths and relax. Do not stress about adopting all the habits mentioned in this book at once. Stress is the opposite of what we want to accomplish, right? If you only change one or two things in your life, you've already made amazing progress.

Aim to make changes in your life because you have the freedom to do so; by choice, not by compulsion. Make changes to live healthier and be more grounded, and happy—whatever that means to you.

Be patient with yourself while you are in the transitional phase. It takes time to adopt a new habit. You'll make mistakes, especially in the beginning when you forget or simply don't want to do what you signed up for.

As long as avoidance and inaction don't become habits, you're going to be okay.

I am very grateful you chose my book over the many other books out there. I'm truly hoping I could deliver to you at least one good idea to start working upon.

Reference

Bergland, Christopher. Oxytocin Ain't Behavin' How Scientists Thought It Would. Psychology Today. 2017. https://www.psychologytoday.com/blog/the-athletes-way/201709/oxytocin-aint-behavin-how-scientists-thought-it-would

Bergland, Cristopher. The Neurochemicals Of Happiness. Psychology Today. 2012. https://www.psychologytoday.com/blog/the-athletes-way/201211/the-neurochemicals-happiness

Cacioppo, John T. Ito, Tiffany A. Larsen Jeff T. Smith, N Kyle. Negative Information Weighs More Heavily on the Brain: The Negativity Bias in Evaluative Categorizations. Citeseerx. 1998. http://citeseerx.ist.psu.edu/viewdoc/download?doi=10.1.1.570.6133&rep=rep1&type=pdf

Chris C. Streeter, Whitfield, Theodore H. Owen, Liz. Rein, Tasha. Karri, Surya K. Yakhkind, Aleksandra. Perlmutter, Ruth. Prescot, Andrew. Renshaw, Perry F. Ciraulo, Domenic A. Jensen, J. Eric. Effects of Yoga Versus Walking on Mood, Anxiety, and Brain GABA Levels: A Randomized Controlled

Reference

MRS Study. NCBI. 2010. https://www.ncbi.nlm.nih.gov/pmc/articles/PMC3111147/

Cooley, Jami. Dopamine Deficiency: Ways to Naturally Overcome Depression. University Health News. 2017. https://universityhealthnews.com/daily/depression/8-natural-dopamine-boosters-to-overcome-depression/

Csikszentmihalyi, Mihaly. Flow: The Psychology Of Optimal Experience. Harper Perennial Modern Classics. 2008.

Duhigg, Charles. The Power Of Habit. Random House. 2012.

Gollowitzer, Peter. Introduction. NYU Psychology. 2017. http://www.psych.nyu.edu/gollwitzer/

Hampton, Debbie. Neuroplasticity: The 10 Fundamentals Of Rewiring Your Brain. Reset. 2015. http://reset.me/story/neuroplasticity-the-10-fundamentals-of-rewiring-your-brain/

Health Publishing, Harvard. Pedometers Motivate People To Exercise. Harvard Health Publishing. 2009. https://www.health.harvard.edu/press_releases/pedometers-motivate-people-to-exercise

Hur, Julia. Koo, Minjung. Hofmann, Wilhelm. When Temptations Come Alive: How Anthropomorphization Undermines Consumer Self-Control. NA - Advances in Consumer Research Volume 41, eds. Simona Botti and Aparna Labroo, Duluth, MN : Association for Consumer Research. 2013. http://www.acrwebsite.org/volumes/v41/acr_v41_14556.pdf

Leroy, Sophie. Why Is It so Hard to Do My Work? Citeerx. 2009. http://citeseerx.ist.psu.edu/viewdoc/download?doi=10.1.1.18

3.1776&rep=rep1&type=pdf

Lifelong Learning Council Queensland Inc. What is lifelong learning? Lifelong Learning Council Queensland Inc. 2016. http://www.llcq.org.au/01_cms/details.asp?ID=12

Manson, Mark. 3 Important Life Skills Nobody Ever Taught You. Mark Manson. 2016. https://markmanson.net/life-skills

Manson, Mark. The Most Important Skill In Life. Mark Manson. 2017. https://markmanson.net/most-important-skill-in-life

Martin, Lauren. Scientists Say It Only Takes 66 Days To Change Your Life, If You're Strong Enough. Elite Daily. 2014. https://www.elitedaily.com/life/motivation/need-stop-bad-habit-need-66-days/784244

McGraw, Kenneth O. Fiala, Jirina. Undermining the Zeigarnik effect: Another hidden cost of reward. Online Library. Journal Of Personality. 1982. http://onlinelibrary.wiley.com/doi/10.1111/j.1467-6494.1982.tb00745.x/abstract;jsessionid=906BB10F2BC06986251AECBD89007203.d03t03

Mitchell, Jason. Macrae, C. Neil. Tait, Kristen A. McNamara Diana L. Golubickis, Marius. Topalidis, Palvos P. Christian, Brittany M. Turning I into me: Imagining your future self. Consciousness And Cognition. 2015. http://jasonmitchell.fas.harvard.edu/Papers/Macrae_imaginingFuture_self_2015.pdf

Nass, Clifford. The Myth Of Multitasking. NPR. 2013. https://www.npr.org/2013/05/10/182861382/the-myth-of-multitasking

Newport, Cal. So Good They Can't Ignore You. Grand Central Publishing. 2012.

Reference

René, Jamila. Top 10 Tips to Practice Moderation. No Nonsense Nutritionist. 2015. http://www.nononsensenutritionist.com/12monthchallenge/month-4-nourish/4-nourish-week-3/

Sherman, Jeremy E. The Secret to Happiness and Compassion: Low Expectations. Psychology Today. 2014. https://www.psychologytoday.com/blog/ambigamy/201408/the-secret-happiness-and-compassion-low-expectations

Stoppler, Melissa Conrad. Pain and Stress: Endorphins: Natural Pain and Stress Fighters. Medicinet. 2017. https://www.medicinenet.com/script/main/art.asp?articlekey=55001

Sullivan, Bob. Thompson, Hugh. Brain, interrupted. The New York Times. 2013. http://www.nytimes.com/2013/05/05/opinion/sunday/a-focus-on-distraction.html

Trass, Ken. The brain and workplace motivation. Law Society. 2016. https://www.lawsociety.org.nz/lawtalk/lawtalk-archives/issue-881/the-brain-and-workplace-motivation

Young, Simon N. How to increase serotonin in the human brain without drugs. NCBI. 2007. https://www.ncbi.nlm.nih.gov/pmc/articles/PMC2077351/

Endnotes

Chapter 1: How Are Habits Created?

1   Jabr, Ferris. Does Thinking Really Hard Burn More Calories? Scientific American. 2012. https://www.scientificamerican.com/article/thinking-hard-calories/
2   Duhigg, Charles. The Power Of Habit. Random House. 2012.
3   Martin, Lauren. Scientists Say It Only Takes 66 Days To Change Your Life, If You're Strong Enough. Elite Daily. 2014. https://www.elitedaily.com/life/motivation/need-stop-bad-habit-need-66-days/784244

Chapter 3: Jump off the Expectation Train

1   Manson, Mark. The Most Important Skill In Life. Mark Manson. 2017. https://markmanson.net/most-important-skill-in-life
2   Sherman, Jeremy E. The Secret to Happiness and Compassion: Low Expectations. Psychology Today. 2014. https://www.

psychologytoday.com/blog/ambigamy/201408/the-secret-happiness-and-compassion-low-expectations

Chapter 4: Self-Discipline

1   Mitchell, Jason. Macrae, C. Neil. Tait, Kristen A. McNamara Diana L. Golubickis, Marius. Topalidis, Palvos P. Christian, Brittany M. Turning I into me: Imagining your future self. Consciousness And Cognition. 2015. http://jasonmitchell.fas.harvard.edu/Papers/Macrae_imaginingFuture_self_2015.pdf
2   Hur, Julia. Koo, Minjung. Hofmann, Wilhelm. When Temptations Come Alive: How Anthropomorphization Undermines Consumer Self-Control. NA - Advances in Consumer Research Volume 41, eds. Simona Botti and Aparna Labroo, Duluth, MN : Association for Consumer Research. 2013. http://www.acrwebsite.org/volumes/v41/acr_v41_14556.pdf

Chapter 5: Procrastination

1   Trass, Ken. The brain and workplace motivation. Law Society. 2016. https://www.lawsociety.org.nz/lawtalk/lawtalk-archives/issue-881/the-brain-and-workplace-motivation
2   McGraw, Kenneth O. Fiala, Jirina. Undermining the Zeigarnik effect: Another hidden cost of reward. Online Library. Journal Of Personality. 1982. http://onlinelibrary.

wiley.com/doi/10.1111/j.1467-6494.1982.tb00745.x/abstract;j
sessionid=906BB10F2BC06986251AECBD89007203.d03t03

3   Robbins, Tony.

Chapter 6: Productivity Booster Habits

1   Health Publishing, Harvard. Pedometers Motivate People To Exercise. Harvard Health Publishing. 2009. https://www.health.harvard.edu/press_releases/pedometers-motivate-people-to-exercise

2   Cacioppo, John T. Ito, Tiffany A. Larsen Jeff T. Smith, N Kyle. Negative Information Weighs More Heavily on the Brain: The Negativity Bias in Evaluative Categorizations. Citeseerx. 1998. http://citeseerx.ist.psu.edu/viewdoc/download?doi=10.1.1.570.6133&rep=rep1&type=pdf

3   Gollowitzer, Peter. Introduction. NYU Psychology. 2017. http://www.psych.nyu.edu/gollwitzer/

Chapter 8: Forget Multi-Tasking

1   Sullivan, Bob. Thompson, Hugh. Brain, interrupted. The New York Times. 2013. http://www.nytimes.com/2013/05/05/opinion/sunday/a-focus-on-distraction.html

2   Leroy, Sophie. Why Is It so Hard to Do My Work? Citeerx. 2009. http://citeseerx.ist.psu.edu/viewdoc/download?doi=10.1.1.183.1776&rep=rep1&type=pdf

Endnotes

3   Nass, Clifford. The Myth Of Multitasking. NPR. 2013. https://www.npr.org/2013/05/10/182861382/the-myth-of-multitasking
4   Csikszentmihalyi, Mihaly. Flow: The Psychology Of Optimal Experience. Harper Perennial Modern Classics. 2008.
5   Newport, Cal. So Good They Can't Ignore You. Grand Central Publishing. 2012.

Chapter 9: Happiness Boosters

1   Bergland, Cristopher. The Neurochemicals Of Happiness. Psychology Today. 2012. https://www.psychologytoday.com/blog/the-athletes-way/201211/the-neurochemicals-happiness
2   Cooley, Jami. Dopamine Deficiency: Ways to Naturally Overcome Depression. University Health News. 2017. https://universityhealthnews.com/daily/depression/8-natural-dopamine-boosters-to-overcome-depression/
3   Stoppler, Melissa Conrad. Pain and Stress: Endorphins: Natural Pain and Stress Fighters. Medicinet. 2017. https://www.medicinenet.com/script/main/art.asp?articlekey=55001
4   Butler, Natalie. 7 Foods That Could Boost Your Serotonin: The Serotonin Diet. Health Line. 2018. https://www.healthline.com/health/healthy-sleep/foods-that-could-boost-your-serotonin#turkey
5   Young, Simon N. How to increase serotonin in the human brain without drugs. NCBI. 2007. https://www.ncbi.nlm.nih.

gov/pmc/articles/PMC2077351/

6　Bergland, Christopher. Oxytocin Ain't Behavin' How Scientists Thought It Would. Psychology Today. 2017. https://www.psychologytoday.com/blog/the-athletes-way/201709/oxytocin-aint-behavin-how-scientists-thought-it-would

7　Chris C. Streeter, Whitfield, Theodore H. Owen, Liz. Rein, Tasha. Karri, Surya K. Yakhkind, Aleksandra. Perlmutter, Ruth. Prescot, Andrew. Renshaw, Perry F. Ciraulo, Domenic A. Jensen, J. Eric. Effects of Yoga Versus Walking on Mood, Anxiety, and Brain GABA Levels: A Randomized Controlled MRS Study. NCBI. 2010. https://www.ncbi.nlm.nih.gov/pmc/articles/PMC3111147/

8　Cohen, Joe. Top 15 Natural Ways to Increase GABA. Self Hacked. 2017. https://selfhacked.com/blog/natural-ways-to-increase-gaba/

Chapter 10: Success Habits

1　Manson, Mark. 3 Important Life Skills Nobody Ever Taught You. Mark Manson. 2016. https://markmanson.net/life-skills

2　Lifelong Learning Council Queensland Inc. What is lifelong learning? Lifelong Learning Council Queensland Inc. 2016. http://www.llcq.org.au/01_cms/details.asp?ID=12

3　Hampton, Debbie. Neuroplasticity: The 10 Fundamentals Of Rewiring Your Brain. Reset. 2015. http://reset.me/story/neuroplasticity-the-10-fundamentals-of-rewiring-your-brain/